The Raccoon Philosopher

by Danai Gagne-Apostolidou
and
Judith Thomas-Solomon

inspired by Martin Buber's
Ten Rungs: Hassidic Sayings

An original mini-musical in mixed and irregular meters
for upper elementary grades, with preparatory activities
for singing, moving, playing of recorders and
Orff instruments, and creating.

SMC 566

(In the U.S.: STAP 566)

SCHOTT

Mainz • London • Madrid • New York • Paris • Prague • Tokyo • Toronto

The authors and publisher would like to thank The Balkin Agency for granting permission—on behalf of the Estate of Martin Buber—for the nonexclusive English language rights to reproduce an adapted version of "Seven Virtues of a Thief" from Buber's TEN RUNGS: HASSIDIC SAYINGS, published by Kensington Books.

SMC 566
(In the U.S.: STAP 566)
ISMN   M-60001-040-0
EAN/ISMN   9790600010400
ISBN   1-902455-18-5

Design, typesetting, and music engraving by William Holab

This book is dedicated to our respective children:
Alicia Melia Gagne and Christopher James Thomas,
who have travelled uniquely through life,
surprise and delight a constant in their "mixed meter" journeys;
and to our students, who give unlimited mixtures of energy and love.

Contents

ACKNOWLEDGMENTS

This work is a loving tribute to Carl Orff and Gunild Keetman. Together they bonded philosophies of teaching with astonishing creativity and a dazzling sense of invention. The result of their work is a gift not only to children of the world, but also to teachers. The materials found in their *Music for Children* publications have elevated elemental music to a prominent position in American music education. They developed inventive, tasteful, timeless, distinctive musical models, all the while asking teachers and students to collaborate in the creative process. We are profoundly grateful to Orff and Keetman because we have taken their comprehensive invitation to invent with open-ended possibility, and offer it to all students and teachers who perform *The Raccoon Philosopher*. As the Orff-Schulwerk scholar Werner Thomas instructs us in his introduction to Keetman's *Elementaria*, "For working with Schulwerk does not entail the study and performance of melodies and songs with ready-made accompaniments, but rather a continuous *ars inveniendi*, a spontaneous art of discovery with a hundred ways and a thousand possible structures."*

Anne Fennell is a gifted teacher who understands the importance of the collaborative process. She joined us in this project with her usual fearless enthusiasm and daunting expertise, bringing this musical to her "Zoom" percussion group and upper grade students of the Vista Academy of Performing Arts, Vista, California, Rodney Goldenburg, former Principal. We are indebted to them all.

Without Carolee Stewart, who first recognized the vision of our raccoons, there would be no musical. We are appreciative for her encouragement as well as her inspired and able honing.

Karen Petty's technological skills were invaluable in helping provide intelligible scores, and we are grateful for her cheerful and effective savvy.

Finally, we wish to acknowledge our husbands, David Gagne and Josef Solomon, who were uncomplaining in their understanding of our schedule through many work weekends, and who were "virtuous" in their support.

Danai Gagne-Apostolidou
Judith Thomas-Solomon

* Werner Thomas, introduction to *Elementaria* by Gunild Keetman, translated by Margaret Murray (London: Schott and Co. Ltd., 1974), page 13.

FOREWARD

The Raccoon Philosopher was inspired by thoughts on virtue by Martin Buber from *Ten Rungs: Hassidic Sayings*.[1] Our adaptation deals with those virtues transferred to the raccoon species. There are ways in which they can instruct us:

- They and those who work with them love one another.
- They do their service quietly by night.
- What they do not finish the first night, they devote to the next.
- What they take they also give up easily.
- They endure hardships, and it matters nothing to them.
- They like their lives and would not exchange them for any other.

The book is organized in two sections. *Section One* provides a series of rhythmic and musical preparations in mixed and irregular meters (with emphasis on 7/8), based on excerpts from *The Raccoon Philosopher*. Ideas are explored for studying specific meters to be moved, played and sung within the mini-musical. Finally, extensions are suggested for other curricular uses under "interdisciplinary connections."

Section Two is the complete mini-musical, *The Raccoon Philosopher*, which embraces mixed and irregular meter concepts, along with playing, singing, moving and creating. This section also includes staging and costuming suggestions, speech play, songs, movement/choreography ideas and Orff orchestrations.

In both sections, true to the Orff-Schulwerk philosophy, it is the authors' intent that the process be engaging and open-ended, and that it be treated as importantly as the materials that are provided. We therefore invite students and teachers not only to enjoy the mini-musical suggestions, but also to revel in the preparatory work, where their ideas may ultimately enhance and enliven the final performance.

ON IRREGULAR AND MIXED METERS

Irregular meter is any asymmetrical meter that contains metric groupings of 2 and 3 beats. Examples are 5/8 or 5/4 (2-3, or 3-2); 7/8 or 7/4 (2-2-3, 2-3-2, etc.); 9/8 or 9/4 (2-2-2-3, 2-3-2-2, etc.). Mixed meter is combinations of two or more different meters occurring consecutively, such as a measure of 4/4 followed by a measure of 2/4 and a measure of 3/8.

While irregular meters are less common in American folk music, they can be found abundantly in music of other cultures, such as Greek, German, Balkan, Eastern European and Latin American, to name a few. For example, 7/8 meter, so frequently found in modern Greek folk music, has its roots in Ancient Greece, where poetry and meter were interdependent, particularly in epic and tragic poetry. Thus it is believed that the poetic meter consisting of "one long and two short" syllables led to the origins of 7/8 meter. We also find 7/8 in many Greek dances such as "Kalamatianos" and its variations, "Karagouna," and the "Syrti" dances from the Aegean Islands.

5/4 meter is also found in Greek dances such as "Tsakonikos."[2] Bulgarian music celebrates 11/8, and wonderful examples of this and other irregular meters are in such Bulgarian traditional and contemporary music as that found on the recordings, "Le Mystere des Voix Bulgares."[3]

American jazz has embraced meters of 5 and 7 playfully as found in the well-known "Take Five" and "Unsquare Dance" (in 7) by Dave Brubeck, and "Circle Song Seven" by Bobby McFerrin.

Mixed meter, while more of a compositional tool, can be found in some folk music, such as the Bavarian "Zweifacher" and "Driefacher" dances. These became the inspiration for Gunild Keetman's "Time Change Dances."[4] There are many good examples of mixed meters for classroom use in the repertoire of the 20th and 21st centuries. Contemporary composer Steve Reich employs mixed meter in much of his music; *Tehillim* is one example. Composers Stephen Sondheim and Leonard Bernstein used the technique widely in such works as *Into the Woods* and *West Side Story*, respectively.

The vitality ignited by irregular and mixed meters provided us with the impetus to create *The Raccoon Philosopher*. We hope the preparatory lessons and mini-musical become the springboard that moves teachers and students to a new appreciation of the power and pleasure of rhythmical asymmetry.

THE RACCOON IS…

…a carnivorous mammal of the genus Procyon, found in the United States, Canada, and Central and South America. The head of the raccoon is broad, with an outstanding mask-like marking around the dark eyes; the rest of the face is pale gray with white whiskers and tapers to a pointed muzzle. It has short and erect ears. Raccoons are plump, with long fur and bushy tails that are decorated with six or seven dark rings. Their short legs end with paws having five toes and naked soles on which they walk with heels touching the ground, not unlike humans. They are grayish-brown in their fur above and light gray underneath.

Raccoons in the United States usually live in trees, near ponds, in forests or close to civilization. During the night they hunt for poultry, mice, insects, fish, frogs or human garbage. Occasionally they eat nuts and wild fruit, and they are skillful swimmers. Northern raccoons spend the winter in dens, usually in a hollow tree in a state of torpor, and emerge during warm periods. Each spring, females bear from four to six young in a single litter, which lives and travels as a group for about a year.

THE TEACHING GOALS OF *THE RACCOON PHILOSOPHER* ARE…
- To afford students opportunities to read, explore, move and have experiences with mixed and irregular meters in a playful and engaging way.
- To give students a role in the creation of the mini-musical through invented speech additions, original choreographies and other creations developed in Sections One and Two.
- To encourage students to find ways of applying mixed and irregular meters in other classroom situations.
- To familiarize students with stage terms and vocabulary.
- To acquaint students with Martin Buber's distinctive ways of thinking, hopefully encouraging them to consider sentient creatures with new understanding.

INSTRUMENTARIUM AND INSTRUMENT ABBREVIATIONS

V	Voice
CM	Counter-Melody
SR	Soprano Recorder
SG	Soprano Glockenspiel
AG	Alto Glockenspiel
SX	Soprano Xylophone
AX	Alto Xylophone
SM	Soprano Metallophone
AM	Alto Metallophone
FC	Finger Cymbals
Cym.	Cymbal
CB	Cow Bell
Tamb.	Tambourine
Bell Tree	Bell Tree
Wind Chime	Wind Chime
WB	Wood Block
S.St.	Slapstick (Whip)
Gui.	Guiro
Rat.	Ratchet
Cab.	Cabasa
TB	Temple Blocks
HD	Hand Drum
MD	Medium Drum
LD	Large Drum
Bon.	Bongo
Con.	Conga
Bot.	Small Bottle
Jug	Large Plastic Water Jug
Lid	Garbage Pail Lid
HC	Hand Clap
FS	Feet Stomp
Bag	Large Bag
Cups	Cups
BX	Bass Xylophone
BM	Bass Metallophone
CBB	Contra Bass Bars (D, E, B)
Timp.	Timpani
Vc.	Violoncello

Endnotes

1 Martin Buber, *Ten Rungs: Hassidic Sayings* (New York: Schocken Books, 1947).
2 "Kalamatianos" and "Tsakonikos" can be found in the Greek edition of Orff-Schulwerk, *Griechische Kinderlieder und Tänze*, by Polyxene Mathéy (London: Schott Music Corporation, 1963).
3 "The Mysterious Bulgarian Voices," 2 volumes, the Bulgarian State Radio and Television Female Vocal Choir, recorded in Bulgaria by Marcel Cellier, Electra/Asylum/Nonesuch Records 9 79201-4.
4 Carl Orff and Gunild Keetman, *Orff-Schulwerk: Music for Children*, Volume III, adapted by Margaret Murray (London: Schott and Co. Ltd., 1963), page 100.

Section One

Preparatory Sequences
Based on Excerpts
from the Mini-Musical
The Raccoon Philosopher

Preparatory Sequence Leading to *Take My Hand*
Playing with Groups of Seven Beats:

Invite students to:

1. Speak the following phrase, clapping the accents on beats 1, 3, 5 (observe groups of 2, 2, 3)

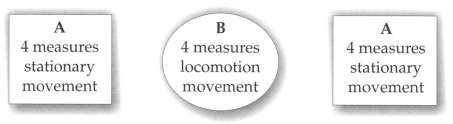

shad - ow   shad - ow   mys - ter - y

2. Add movement on the accents, standing in one place. Add locomotion.
3. Vary the dynamics in the speech and movement, e.g. LOUD = large; SOFT = small.
4. Create a choreography in ABA form using stationary and locomotion movement:

| **A**
4 measures
stationary
movement | **B**
4 measures
locomotion
movement | **A**
4 measures
stationary
movement |

5. Explore ways to play the words "shadow, shadow, mystery" on the body.

chest
clap
slap right leg
slap left leg

6. In the same way, play with the groups of 3, 2, 2, "mystery, shadow, shadow," e.g.:

clap
slap right leg
slap left leg

7. Decide how many times each pattern will be repeated. Combine speech, movement, body percussion, and form into a class-created performance piece. Find a place for it within the mini-musical!

Interdisciplinary Connections

Apply 7/8 meter to the names of Greek gods, in conjunction with a Greek history unit (possibly serving as preparation for Greek dances in 7/8). For example:

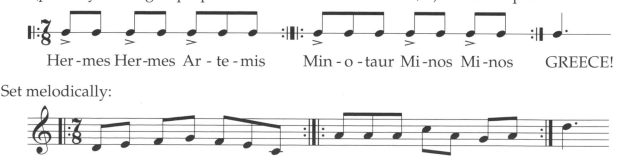

Her -mes Her -mes Ar - te -mis   Min - o -taur Mi -nos Mi -nos   GREECE!

Set melodically:

Her -mes Her -mes Ar - te -mis   Min - o -taur Mi -nos Mi -nos   GREECE!

Apply to Roman gods. For example:

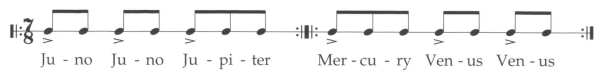

Ju - no   Ju - no   Ju - pi - ter   Mer - cu - ry   Ven - us   Ven - us

Preparatory Sequence Leading to *Service by Night*

Playing with the Dorian mode:

In order for students to enjoy improvising in diatonic modes, they must clearly know where the main pitches of the mode lie in order to emphasize these important pitches on the strong beats of their melodies. These tones are 1, 3 and 5, falling on D, F and A, respectively. The Dorian mode sounds like a natural minor scale because of the minor third interval between D and F. B♮, the raised sixth degree, distinguishes it as the Dorian mode.

1. Invite students to improvise a sung, two-tone melody on D and F using the 7/8 rhythms below:

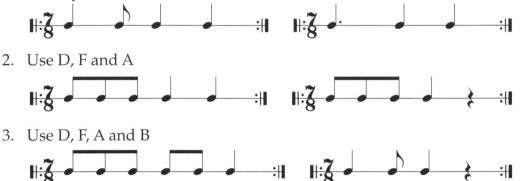

2. Use D, F and A

3. Use D, F, A and B

4. Repeat the task on Orff instruments. Using D, F, A and B, the metals ask a question and the woods answer.

5. Continue the game, adding the passing tones gradually: E, G, and C. If students have difficulty basing their melodies on the 1, 3 and 5 tones of the mode, a temporary marker can be placed on these instrument bars as a reminder. Example of question (Q) and answer (A) using D, A and B:

Example using D, F, A and B:

Example using the main pitches, sixth scale degree and passing tones E and G, consciously landing on tones 1, 3 or 5 on the accented beats:

The teacher or students might add a bordun accompaniment:

6. Create an eight-bar percussion section in 7/8 using these small percussion, in any combination: wood block, guiro, finger cymbals, bongos, conga, timpani, ratchet, tambourine.
7. Create an ABA piece in 7/8, Dorian mode, using barred instruments—small percussion—barred instruments. Perhaps the resulting piece might work as another contrasting section in *Service by Night*.

Preparatory Sequence Leading to *There's a Can Down the Way*

1. While speaking the text, invite students to conduct a four-beat pattern two times, changing to 7/8 two times, then changing to 6/8 two times:

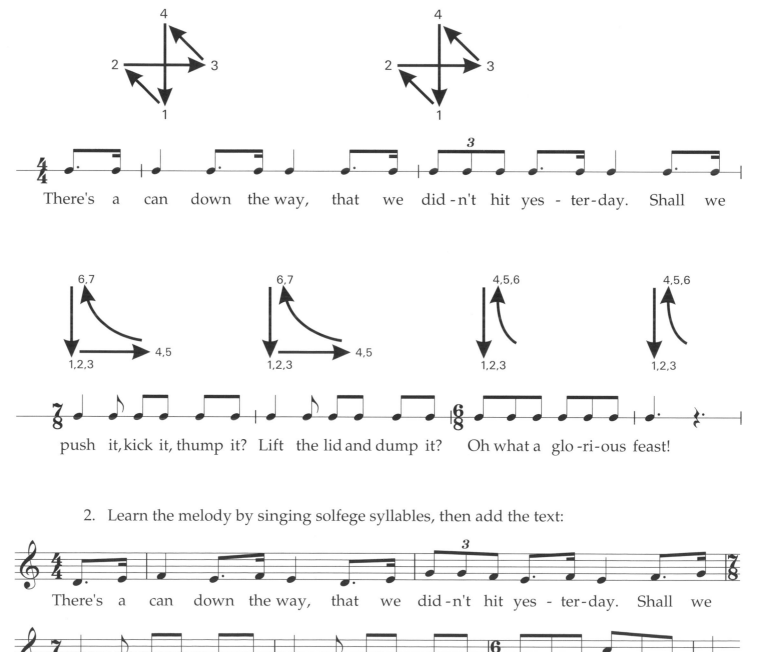

2. Learn the melody by singing solfege syllables, then add the text:

3. Practice the following body percussion patterns with a partner while singing the song:

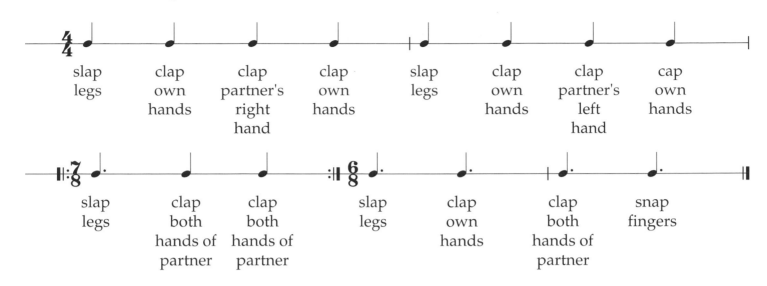

| slap legs | clap own hands | clap partner's right hand | clap own hands | slap legs | clap own hands | clap partner's left hand | cap own hands |

| slap legs | clap both hands of partner | clap both hands of partner | | slap legs | clap own hands | clap both hands of partner | snap fingers |

4. Divide the class into two groups. One group does the above body percussion patterns in pairs. The other group practices the soprano xylophone part on their laps during the 4/4 measures, preparing for the crossover mallet technique. Everyone sings.

Soprano Xylophone

♪ = right hand
♪ = left hand

5. Explore steps that work with 4/4 meter, e.g., step hop step hop; step step step hop; jog jog jog jog. Then explore movements in 7/8 meter on accent words (push, kick, thump, lift, lid, dump, oh, glo, feast) using elbows, knees, palms, hands, feet, etc. Use these ideas to create a choreography for *There's a Can Down the Way*.

Interdisciplinary Connections

Using familiar proverbs, fit them into the respective meters to create mixed meter speech pieces, e.g.:

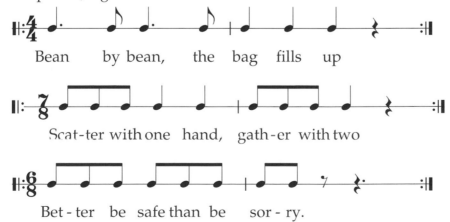

Bean   by bean,   the   bag   fills   up

Scat-ter with one   hand,   gath-er with two

Bet - ter   be safe than be   sor - ry.

9

Preparatory Sequence Leading to *Found Sound Jam*
Words That Make Us Move

1. Invite students to select action words from the list below and move to them:

Locomotion	Stopping Actions
Scurry, skip, hop,	Stop, pause, grip,
slide, leap, loop, spin	perch, freeze

2. Learn the speech pattern below, then set it to motion using ideas from above:

A Section:

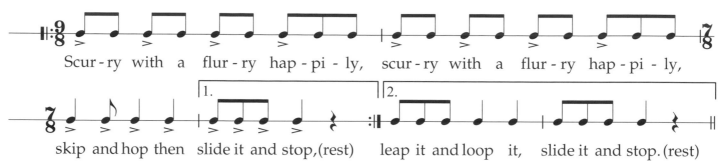

Scur-ry with a flur-ry hap-pi-ly, scur-ry with a flur-ry hap-pi-ly,

skip and hop then slide it and stop, (rest) leap it and loop it, slide it and stop. (rest)

> Invite students to invent a locomotive motion for the 9/8 measure, then shape the rest of their choreography using the locomotion and stopping action words from number 1.

3. Transfer the speech pattern onto large plastic water jugs, small bottles and/or hand claps.
4. Create a group choreography based on the A section of *Found Sound Jam,* ending it with SPIN STEP STEP STOP."
5. Using the word meanings to initiate movement, invite students to find interesting pathways as they chant and move:

B Section

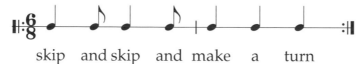

skip and skip and make a turn

Add other dance ideas to the contrasting rondo sections of *Found Sound Jam.*

Interdisciplinary Connections
Invite students to invent color chains to be worked into "woven color pieces" in art class and later, danced:

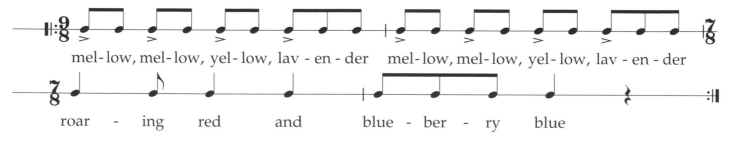

mel-low, mel-low, yel-low, lav-en-der   mel-low, mel-low, yel-low, lav-en-der

roar - ing red and blue-ber-ry blue

> Call attention to the onomatopoeia of specific words, which will help give ideas for movement, e.g., roaring calls for a large, "roaring" movement; "mellow, mellow" suggests a more refined gesture, etc.

Preparatory Sequence Leading to *Night Winds*

Movement Qualities and Phrase Lengths

1. The movement qualities needed for *Night Winds* can be found in six of the Laban* "Basic Effort Movements."
    a. Light and sudden motions (FLICK, DAB)
    b. Light, smooth and slow motions (FLOAT, GLIDE)
    c. Heavy, smooth and slow motions (PRESS, WRING)
2. To the sound of a cymbal played with metal striker or brush, invite students to explore the words "flick and dab" by moving different parts of the body, e.g., hands, head, elbows, shoulders, wrists, knees, etc. Continue exploring the remaining qualities while listening to the cymbal for other movement cues, such as floating to a soft crescendo or pressing to a loud crescendo.
3. In small groups, ask students to develop a short movement composition using one word from each category in number 1 above. The piece can be accompanied by vocal sounds or small percussion appropriate to the movement.
    Example:

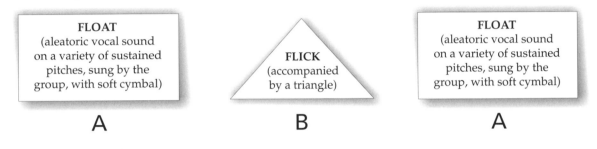

| FLOAT (aleatoric vocal sound on a variety of sustained pitches, sung by the group, with soft cymbal) | FLICK (accompanied by a triangle) | FLOAT (aleatoric vocal sound on a variety of sustained pitches, sung by the group, with soft cymbal) |
| A | B | A |

4. Speak the words of *Night Winds* and apply the movement efforts in a stationary way, changing floor direction at each metric change. Add locomotion to the B section, still exploring PRESS, FLOAT, and GLIDE.

Interdisciplinary Connections

Take the idea of a phrase structure with one measure of 6/8, one of 9/8, and again one of 6/8, and apply it to writing using metaphor, simile, alliteration, onomatopoeia, and adjective.

Ask students to describe special scenes that resonate in their lives, such as a "night beach moment" or "daytime beach experience."

Sea-weed-y sweet-ness, sky vel-vet heav-y, a can-o-py hum-ming with stars.

Surf sounds are play-ing scal-lops of rhy-thms, mys-te-ri-ous mes-sag-es say-ing

* Rudolph Laban, *Modern Educational Dance* (Great Britain: MacDonald & Evans, 1973).

Preparatory Sequence Leading to *The Hunt*
Complementary Rhythms
Explain to the students what constitutes "complementary rhythms" through the following games:

1. **Switch**: In partners, one person (A) plays a steady beat using body percussion while the other (B) creates a simple pattern using quarter and eighth notes. At a prearranged sound, such as a drum beat or triangle, they switch.

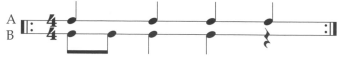

    Play the same game, but A plays a simple pattern and B's task is to play a pattern that is *different* from the A pattern; thus B complements A.

    Increase rhythmic interest and difficulty by using more than one body percussion level.

2. **Move a complement:** In groups of four, partners move in complement to each other while the other two accompany them with drums or other small percussion. Invite students to find sounds that complement each other as well, e.g., drum and woodblock.

    To increase difficulty, add another movement layer and another accompaniment. Invite students to evaluate groups for effective complement, where rhythms and movement are different and therefore complementary.

3. **Timbral complement:** Invite groups of 4 to find instruments that "fit" with each other in contrasting sound and create 2-measure ostinati for each part, assessing within and without the group for effectiveness in timbre difference.

4. **Textural complement:** Invite students to choose more than four complementary instruments and create a tapestry of texture and timbre. Teacher and students together can notate the resulting layered rhythms, being careful to line up the beats vertically and horizontally. See example in *The Hunt*.

Interdisciplinary Connections
Complementary Visual Designs
Study the works of Paul Klee, Alexander Calder, and Joan Miró for complementary visual elements, e.g., lines, curves and shapes used in contrast.

Examples:
*   "Rich Harbor," 1938, Paul Klee: contrasting lines
*   "The Niesen," 1915, Paul Klee: contrasting geometric shapes
*   "Landscape with Yellow Birds," 1923, Paul Klee: contrasting planes, geometric and bird shapes

Translate these designs into complementary rhythm patterns singly, with partners or in small groups.

Section Two

The Raccoon Philosopher,
A MINI-MUSICAL INSPIRED BY
MARTIN BUBER'S WRITINGS
FROM *Ten Rungs: Hasidic Sayings*

ORDER OF SCENES

1. **Introduction and Overture** *Take My Hand*
   Take my hand, don't let the darkness scare you,
   Take my hand, let us both take the dare, you
   Must be strong, even when people chase us,
   Nights are long, only the moon to race us,
   Take my hand.

2. *Service by Night*

   <u>Group 1</u>   <u>Group 2</u>
   Service by night,   Running!
   Service by night,   Prying!
   Service by night,   Hiding!
   Start when it's late.

   Service by night,   Running!
   Service by night,   Prying!
   Service by night,   Hiding!
   This is our fate!

   <u>Tutti</u>
   No one can see us, no one can be us,
   Only the moon and the stars for a light,
   No one can see us, no one can be us,
   Only the darkness and wind in the night.

3. *There's a Can Down the Way*
   There's a can down the way,
   That we didn't hit yesterday.
   Shall we push it, kick it, thump it?
   Lift the lid and dump it?
   OH, WHAT A GLORIOUS FEAST!

   Just to find, what's inside,
   Fills our stomach and fills our pride.
   Shall we push it, kick it, thump it?
   Lift the lid and dump it?
   OH, WHAT A GLORIOUS FEAST!

   <u>Speech:</u>
   Chocolate left on an ice cream cone,
   Raisins stuck to a nearby stone,
   Pieces of bacon and scrambled eggs,
   Succulent scraps of chicken legs.

   Delicate lettuce,
   Burned black beans,
   Peelings from carrots,
   Salad greens.

Easily come by, easily given,
For only the quest are we wholly driven.
OH, WHAT A GLORIOUS FEAST!

4. **Raccoon** *Found Sound Jam*

5. *Night Winds*
Take… heed… slow… speed… paw… right… stop.

Night winds are bringing,
Left-over fragrances singing,
Hard to resist.

Night winds are bringing,
Left-over fragrances singing,
What have we missed?

Sensors deflecting,
Shadows detecting,
Something's not right… MAN IN SIGHT!!!

6. *The Hunt*
(instrumental)

7. *Hunted by People*
Hunted by people,
Chased without cause,
No food in winter,
Frozen paws.

What does it matter,
We're here together.
Hardships can't break us,
Can't break us apart.

Bonded by life,
We all help each other.
Proof of our loving
And loyal hearts.

Coda:
Still we endure,
Still we endure,
Still we endure,
In ev'ry hardship;
And we are together!

7. **Reprise**: *Take My Hand*
Entire Cast

SCRIPT AND STAGING SUGGESTIONS

Cast

Actors/Dancers . . . . minimum of 24

Chorus . . . . any size

Instrumental Ensemble . . . . any size

Flashlight Dancers . . . . approximately 12

Stage Setup

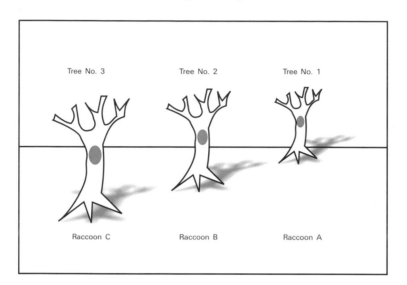

OVERTURE *TAKE MY HAND*

Stage Directions

1. Before the overture begins, three raccoons (A, B and C) creep onto stage left and right toward the trees, wind around the tree trunks and end up hidden behind them in silence.

2. Three groups of approximately seven raccoons are offstage:
   Group 1, offstage left
   Group 2, offstage right
   Group 3, offstage right

3. In mm. 3, 5 and 7 of the Introduction, Raccoons A, B and C appear in tandem in the holes in the trunks of the trees, then disappear.

4. Mm. 9–13, Raccoon A peeks to the left of Tree 1, then moves around the tree to

   the rhythm:

5. Mm. 13–14, Raccoon C reveals its tail to stage right and freezes.

6. Mm. 15–19, Group 2 enters from stage right, grabs Raccoon C's tail and forms a tail chain, moving clockwise. At the same time, Group 3 enters from stage right, moving toward Raccoon B at Tree 2 to play "follow the leader," in movement, working downstage as they copy B. The dialogue begins at the *Subito stop* (end of Introduction, m. 22).

Take My Hand
Overture

Danai Gagne-Apostolidou
and Judith Thomas-Solomon

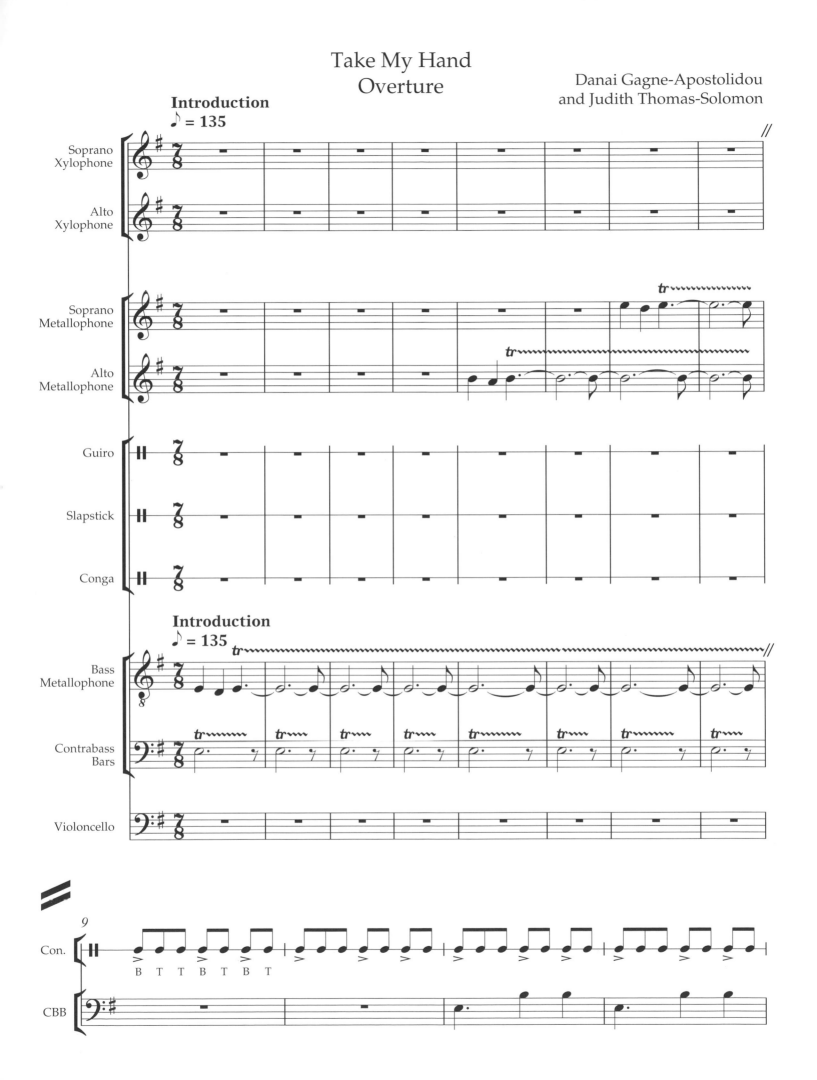

DIALOGUE (OVER SILENCE)

ALL

Look up! What a moon!

SOLO I

What a quiet, moonlit night!

ALL

Makes you reflect! *(group looks to next speaker)*

SOLO 2

Makes you reflect …on life!

SOLO 3

…on … *being*!

SOLO 4

… on being … an animal family with strong ties…

ALL

Yeah … bonded… *(doing "high fives")*

SOLO 4

(thoughtfully) … thinking

SOLO 5

…reflecting

SOLO 6

(with pride at thinking of a large word) Philosophizing!

ALL

(looking at him quizzically) Philosophizing?

SOLO 6

(explaining) … figuring out why it is so good being in a raccoon family. *(Raccoons ponder.)*

SOLO 7

… well, we work together, and…

ALL

… we love one another…

SOLO 8

And together, with hands held *(they do)* nothing can hurt us.

SOLO 9

No one can chase us…

ALL

And nothing in the darkness can scare us.

Take My Hand

24

Take my hand

Take my hand

DIALOGUE AFTER *TAKE MY HAND*

(BM and AM tremolo on "A" under dialogue)

ALL

The moon is higher now

SOLO 9

… gift from the night!

SOLO 10

… illuminates our world

SOLO 11

… we could work by sunlight…

SOLO 12

But service by night keeps us safe!

(tremolo ends)

SERVICE BY NIGHT

Stage Directions

1. At the song's Introduction, form two groups for Voices 1 and 2. Develop stationary movements that reflect the meaning of the words running, prying, and hiding. Consider high, medium, and low levels for movement contrast.
2. On the B section, develop a tiptoeing, locomotive step, moving on the measure accents.
3. On the C section, select solo dancers for the question and answer phrases.
4. End the piece with a loud stage whisper: "shhhhhhhh."

DIALOGUE

Conga begins to play: $\frac{7}{8}$ ♩ ♩ ♩ ♩ ♩ ♩ ♩

After several repeats, this pattern continues as accompaniment to the dialogue.

ALL:

(Spoken quickly, as in the rhythm of the song)
Service by night

SOLO 12

…running

ALL

Service by night

SOLO 13

… prying

ALL

Service by night

SOLO 14

… hiding

ALL

Start when it's late

ALL

Service by night

SOLO 12

…running

ALL

Service by night

SOLO 13

… prying

ALL

Service by night

SOLO 14

… hiding

ALL

This is our fate.

(Conga stops.)

Service by Night

Danai Gagne-Apostolidou
and Judith Thomas-Solomon

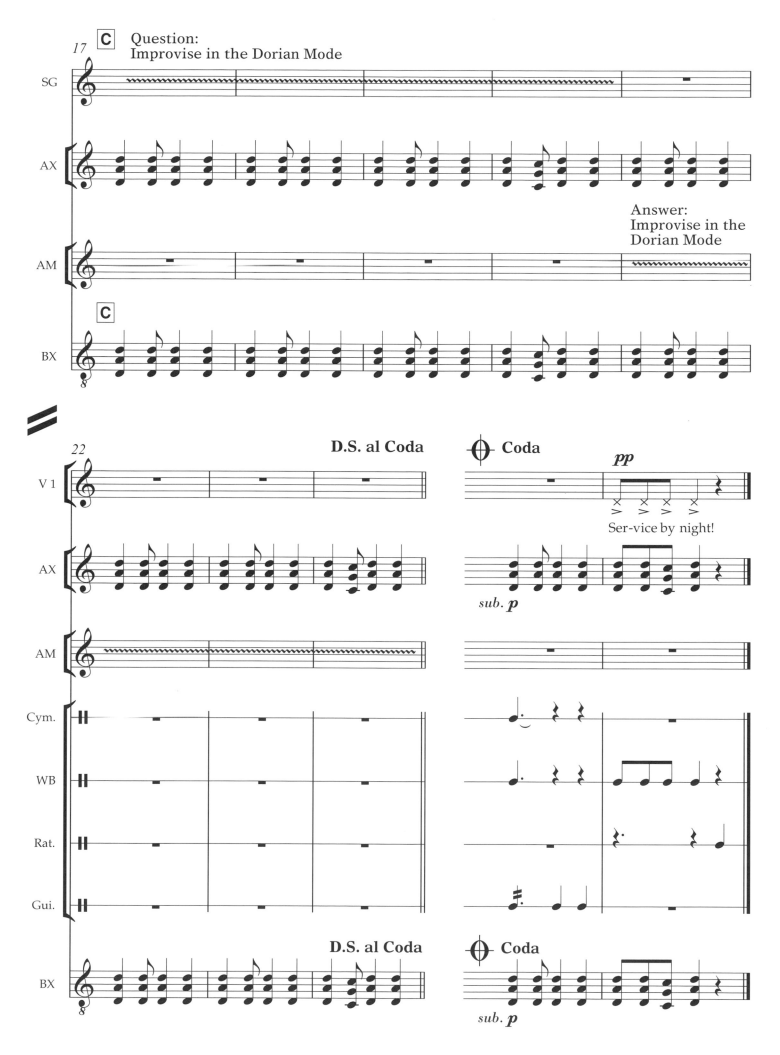

DIALOGUE

SOLO 14

(*noticing sky*) We have to go…   it's almost light!

SOLO 15

… but we're not done yet!

ALL

Shhh. What we cannot complete one night, we come back and finish the next!
(*all say "finish the next" ad lib.*)

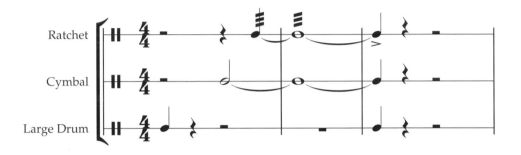

ALL

What was that?!

SOLO 16

(*nonchalant tone*)
Stay calm… it was only a rolling can!

ALL

(*relieved sound*)

SOLO 17

(*imitating nonchalant tone of Solo 16*)
… only a can (*changing tone*) … but a can CAN stand for opportunity!

ALL

Yes! A delicious one!

SOLO 18

Did we go through this can yet? (*a few raccoons investigate it*)

THERE'S A CAN DOWN THE WAY

Stage Directions

1. As raccoons find various foods, they come to the front and split off in different directions away from the cluster of raccoons, eating rapturously.

2. Raccoons tiptoe downstage, facing the audience, approaching the can. Note: Singers should sing in a crisp-dictioned, almost staccato style.

3. Invite students to use the actions words "push, kick, thump, lift, and dump" to define choreographed movements.

4. At "just to find," ask students to develop an "in place" march downstage. Here's an example to try:

    R L R L, stepping in place, making the longest stride on the first "right."

5. **B Section, Introduction:** Hand drum, four measures before food speech. (See mm. 20–23 in the score.) As the hand drum, ratchet, guiro, and conga play softly, the food poem is chanted in 7/8 over the rhythm ensemble.

6. **C Section:** Solos take food poem lines.

7. Create a final "tableau" of all the raccoons, holding the pose for four beats at the end.

There's a Can Down the Way

Danai Gagne-Apostolidou
and Judith Thomas-Solomon

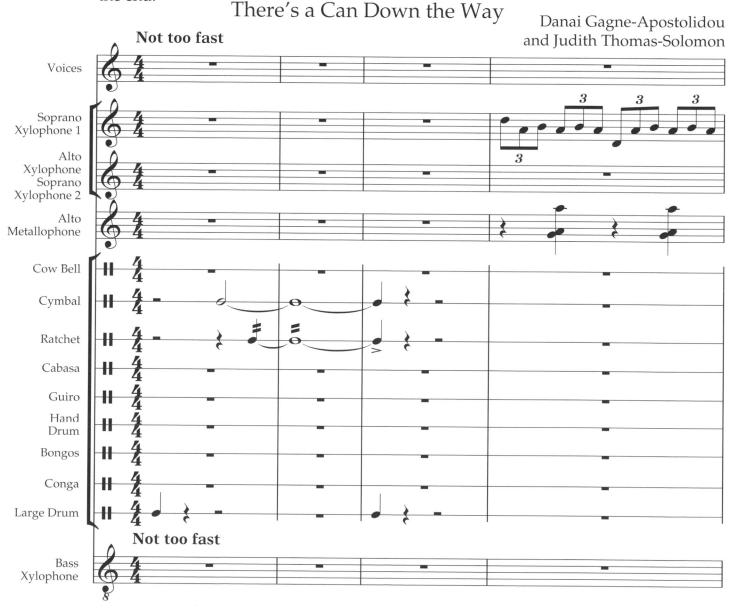

find, what's in-side, Fills our stom-ach and fills our pride. Shall we push it, kick it, thump it?

to Coda

Lift the lid and dump it? Oh, what a glo-ri-ous feast!

to Coda

find, what's in-side, Fills our stom-ach and fills our pride. Shall we push it, kick it, thump it?

Lift the lid and dump it? Oh, what a glo - ri - ous feast!

DIALOGUE (OVER SILENCE)

SOLO 23

Hey! Anybody wanna trade my ice cream cone for a chicken leg?

SOLO 24

(*semi-sarcastically*) Aren't we generous today!

SOLO 25

"Easy come, easy go" … anyone want my carrot peelings?

SOLO 1

I'll trade you for salad greens!

SOLO 2

(*holding his food greedily*) NO one's getting my French bread … Nobody! (*all glower at him*)

SOLO 3

Uh, uh. Not the way it's done around here.

ALL

SHARING is the mark of true friendship!

FOUND SOUND JAM

Stage Directions

1. Raccoon No. 1 picks up a bottle and begins the 7/8 pattern with metal striker. The group slowly turns with interest, as about seven more raccoons wander off to get more bottles to join the pattern.
2. Raccoon No. 2 plays the large bag part and other raccoons join him.
3. Raccoon No. 3 plays the garbage pail lid and is joined by two others.
4. A group of raccoons follows No. 4, who does the hand clapping pattern.
5. Raccoon No. 5 begins the foot stomping pattern and is joined by the others.

Note: Groups of same instruments stand in clusters on the stage for ease of hearing. The only groups moving through space are the clappers and the stompers.

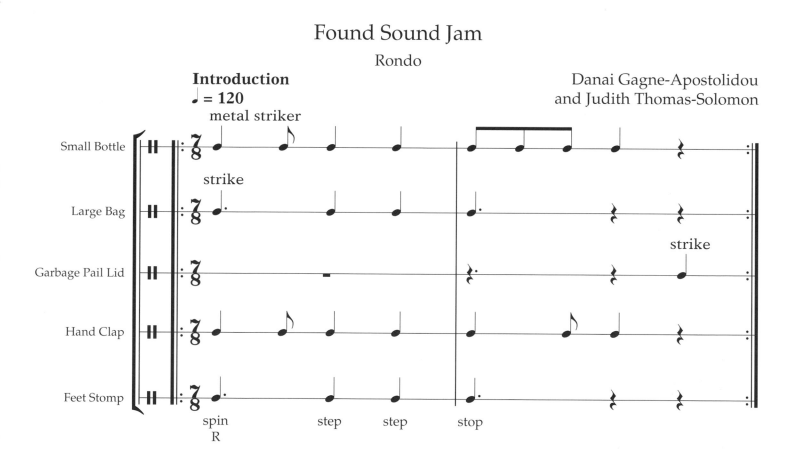

Found Sound Jam

Rondo

Patterns enter one at a time in the order listed, cumulatively. Each pattern plays for four measures before the next part enters. After all parts are in, the whole ensemble plays 2 more times and stops. The **A** section begins immediately.

6. Three large plastic bottle players with stompers.

7. Three cup players, three bottle blowers, and three small lid players break through the groups to perform downstage. As other raccoons listen and look at them attentively, they play the ensemble two times. As section **B** is repeated two more times, dancers either create a fixed choreography or improvise a dance (eight measures).

8. Select a "found sound" instrument from the list below, then improvise for eight meaures and choreograph a short movement composition in 6/8 meter.
   - newspaper
   - crumpled cellophane
   - cup with a squeaky straw (stuck through a plastic lid)
   - scraped coffee cans (with ridges on the sides)
   - shaken match boxes, etc.

C

A la *Stomp* (the long-running Off-Broadway show).

9. With two groups using drums and "found sounds" of their choice, play the 4/4 and 6/8 patterns alternately. Those not playing should improvise with movement. Musicians and movers create a final "tableau" and freeze at the end of the final A section.

D "Play" with interchanging these two patterns using found sounds of your choice.

Roll-ing and roll-ing and step and stop

Repeat **A** Final form: A B A C A D A (Rondo form).

NIGHT WINDS

Stage Direction

Raccoon scarf dancers take scarves from behind trees and hold them hidden in their hands before using them in the dance.

Night Winds

Play softly under dialogue.

Danai Gagne-Apostolidou
and Judith Thomas-Solomon

ALL

Look up! No moon tonight. *(in a tone that remembers the moonlit night)*

SOLO 4

Lost our light.

SOLO 5

That's all right … we're not afraid.

SOLO 6

What is that wonderful fragrance? *(all sniffing)*

SOLO 7

It's like perfume…

ALL

(sniffing) It's *every*where. It's *food*!

SOLO 8

(longingly) Night winds are bringing us fragrances…

SOLO 9

(giving in) Sooo hard to resist!

BACKGROUND MUSIC STOPS.

ALL

(large sigh) Mmmmmmmm.

Stage Directions

1. On first playing, BM and CBB play alone as raccoons tentatively walk around the stage "sniffing."

2. On the second playing, they speak in a stage whisper.

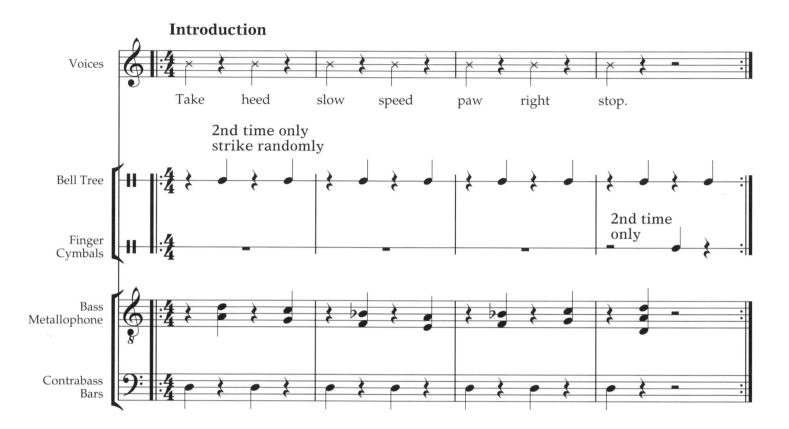

3. **A:** Students decide on a group stationary movement to coordinate with the words "night," "leftover," and "hard," moving in a new direction with each phrase.

4. **B:** Improvise a gliding choreography with a small group using flowing scarves as others sing in place. Hide scarves in hands at the end of **B**.

5. **A':** Find a way to regroup on the stage so that the counter-melody singers can be heard.

6. **B':** Add more dancers with scarves, gliding rapidly and with large, "fortissimo" movements and forceful singing.

7. **A':** Fade… section ends softly and is taken over by a D tremolo on the BM.

THE HUNT

Stage Directions

1. Raccoons divide into two groups for song. Hunters prepare to enter stage left and right at four musical entries. They have flashlights.
2. Groups sing, holding at the fermatas at the end of each phrase, looking furtively about, sensing imminent danger.
3. On the word "sight" of the segue, BX, AX, and SX enter and play twice. They continue under the rest of *The Hunt*.

Note: Hunters can be of the traditional ilk in vests, hats, etc., or "urban," in pajamas, robes, curlers, etc., at the discretion of the students.

Segue to The Hunt

Danai Gagne-Apostolidou
and Judith Thomas-Solomon

Xylophone ostinati continue throughout *The Hunt*. Xylophones play two times before percussion ensemble begins.

4. Four groups of flashlight dancers with approximately three people per group are off stage. Group No. 1 enters from stage left and coordinates lights "on and off" in a group-created choreography as Ensemble 1 begins to play.

5. After two repetitions of the pattern by Ensemble 1, Ensemble 2 begins to play its pattern and Flashlight Group No. 2 enters from stage right.

6. After two repetitions of Ensemble 2's pattern, Ensemble 3 begins and Flashlight Group No. 3 enters from stage left.

7. After two repetitions of Ensemble 3's pattern, Ensembles 4 and 5 begin their patterns and Flashlight Group No. 4 enters from stage right.

8. The full ensemble of instruments and the four flashlight groups continue for another eight measures. In reverse order, instruments and dancers phase out as the raccoons huddle upstage fearfully until there is only the BX tremolo on B playing.

The Hunt

Danai Gagne-Apostolidou
and Judith Thomas-Solomon

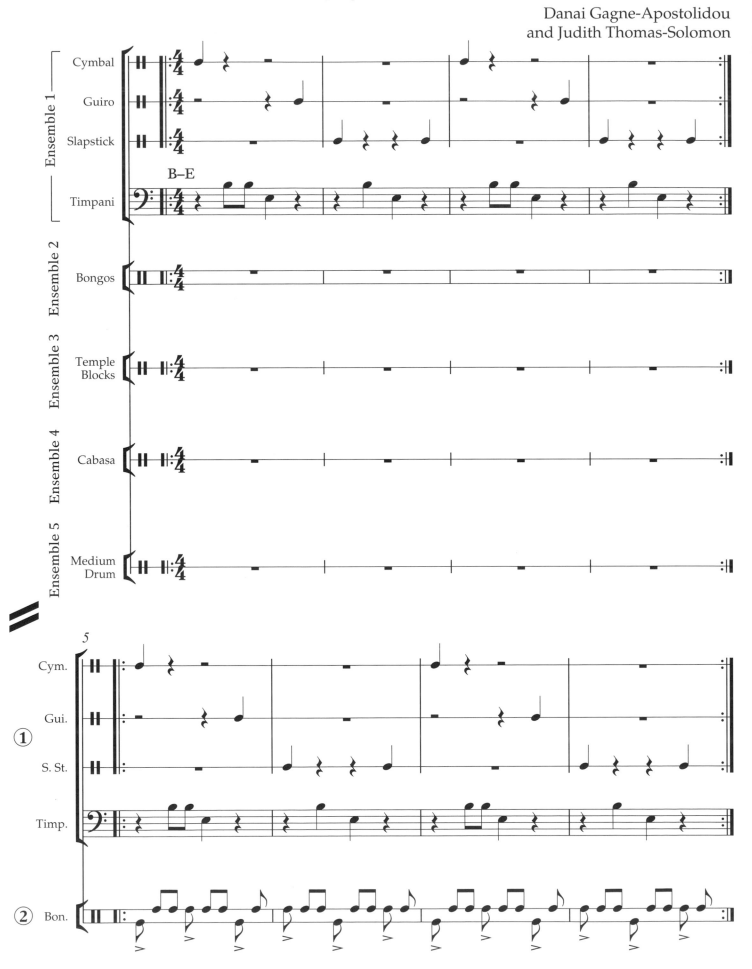

segue

HUNTED BY PEOPLE

Stage Directions

1. After hunters have left, raccoons return timidly in four groups, moving downstage one group at a time, as they sing their respective phrases:
    a. Hunted by people
    b. Chased without cause
    c. No food in winter
    d. Frozen paws

They repeat, moving on their phrase and freezing as other groups sing.

Hunted by People

Danai Gagne-Apostolidou
and Judith Thomas-Solomon

59

2. On the word "paws" sung on the repeat, the AM plays the pattern two times alone.
3. The four groups sing *Hunted by People* two times in unison, then two more times in four-part canon with the entire orchestration: AM, BX 1, BX 2, Timpani.
4. During the solos in the B section, only the AM and BX 1 accompany.
5. Return to A. AX and BM are added to the ensemble. The song is sung over this in four-part canon two more times.
6. Taking a large *ritard* into *Still We Endure,* the B tremolo on the CBB and BM play beneath.

Still We Endure

Bridge to *Take My Hand* (reprise)

Danai Gagne-Apostolidou
and Judith Thomas-Solomon

Take My Hand
Reprise

Danai Gagne-Apostolidou
and Judith Thomas-Solomon